A Home for Every Cat

I0194203

This book belongs to

....

All profits from the sale of this book are donated to
New Beginnings Cat Rescue. Thank you for your support.

Copyright © 2024 Helen Aitchison

The moral right of Helen Aitchison to be identified as the author of the work has been asserted by her in accordance with the Copyright, Designs and Patents Act 1988.
First published in Great Britain in 2024 by Write on the Tyne CIC.
No part of this publication may be reproduced, distributed, or transmitted in any form or by any means, including photocopying, recording or other electrical or mechanical methods, without prior written permission of the author, except in the case of brief quotations embodied in reviews and certain other non-commercial uses permitted by copyright law.

Printed by Amazon

Paperback ISBN: 978-1-7394882-5-3
All images : Ameila Clark-Sutton

Published by Write on the Tyne
www.writeonthetyne.com

It is Saturday, Eric's favourite day of the week. Eric loves Saturdays as his parents, Helen and Paul, are off work and he can spend lots of time with them.

Saturday means Eric can play outside. He can see some of his neighbourhood friends, knowing on his return, he will get a treat and a knee to snuggle up on. Yes, Saturday is definitely the best day of the week.

One Saturday morning, Eric was playing out, having lots of fun exploring the shrubs and trees near his home. He ran in the long green grass, said hello to other cats, and chased butterflies.

Eric felt lucky to live in an area where it was safe to wander, play, and go on an adventure. He hadn't always been so lucky in life.

Later that afternoon, after playing out, Eric curled up on his dad's knee. Hearing the football on TV, he drifted off to sleep, thinking about his old, lonely life before he was adopted.

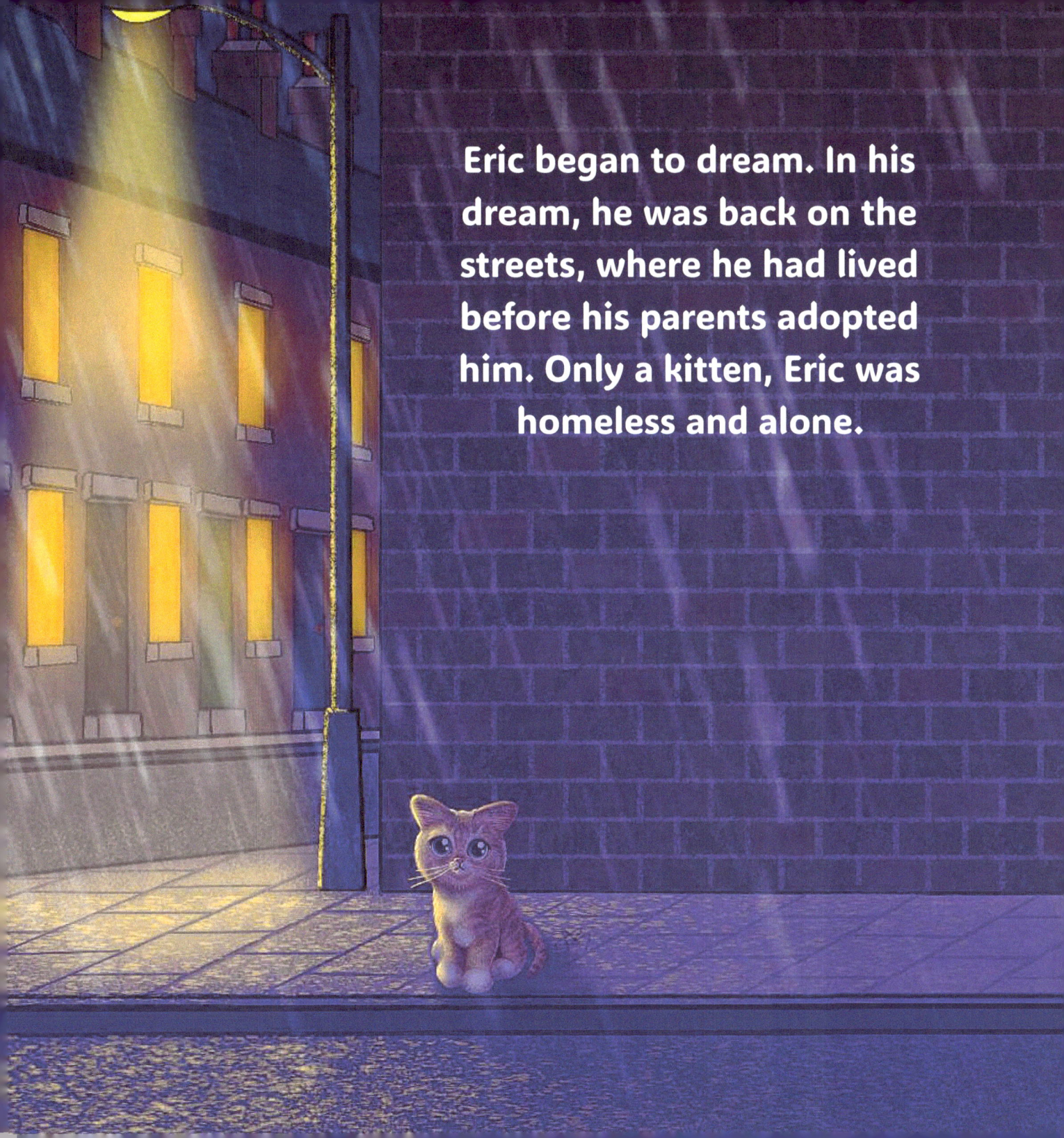

Eric began to dream. In his dream, he was back on the streets, where he had lived before his parents adopted him. Only a kitten, Eric was homeless and alone.

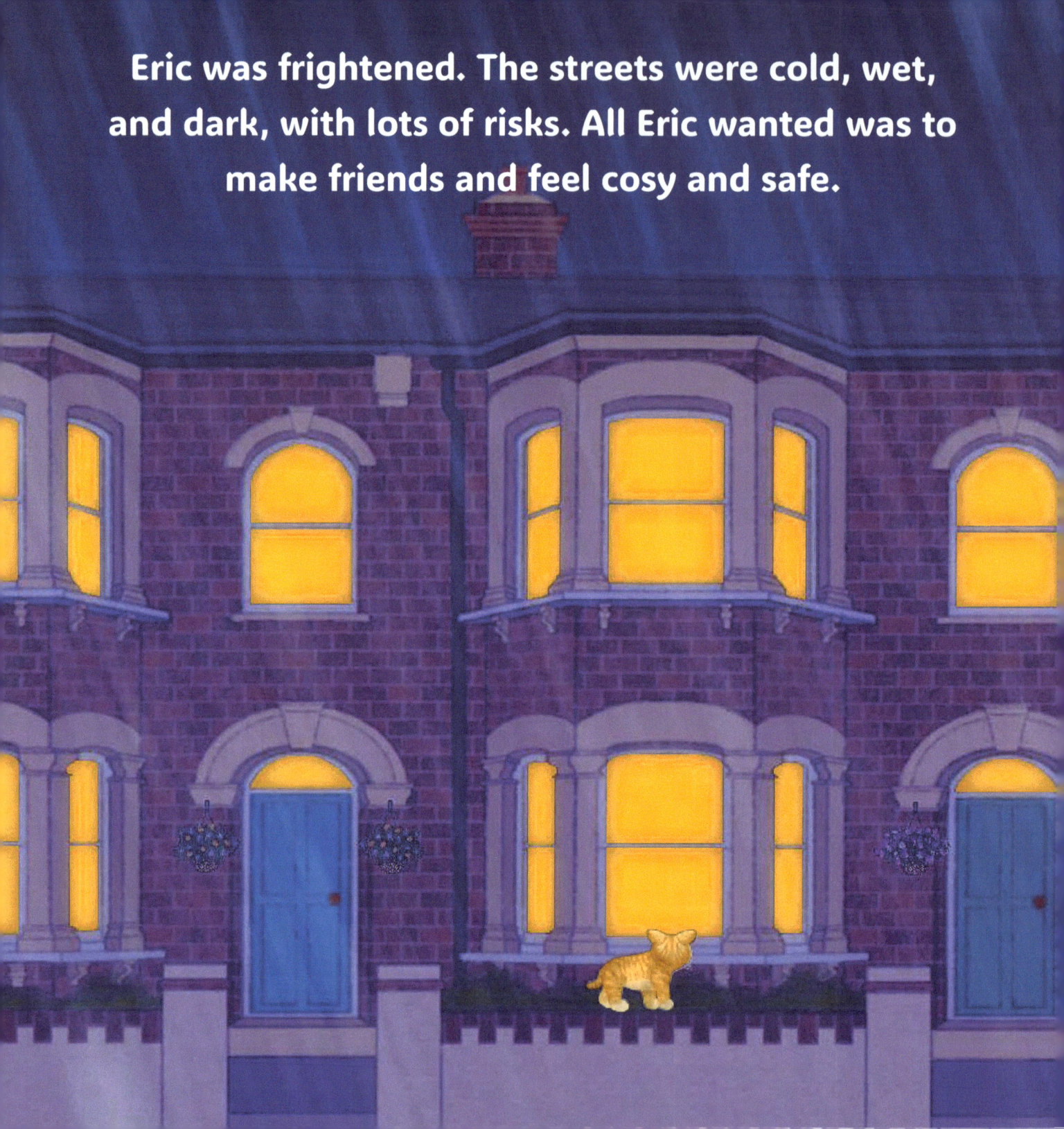
Eric was frightened. The streets were cold, wet, and dark, with lots of risks. All Eric wanted was to make friends and feel cosy and safe.

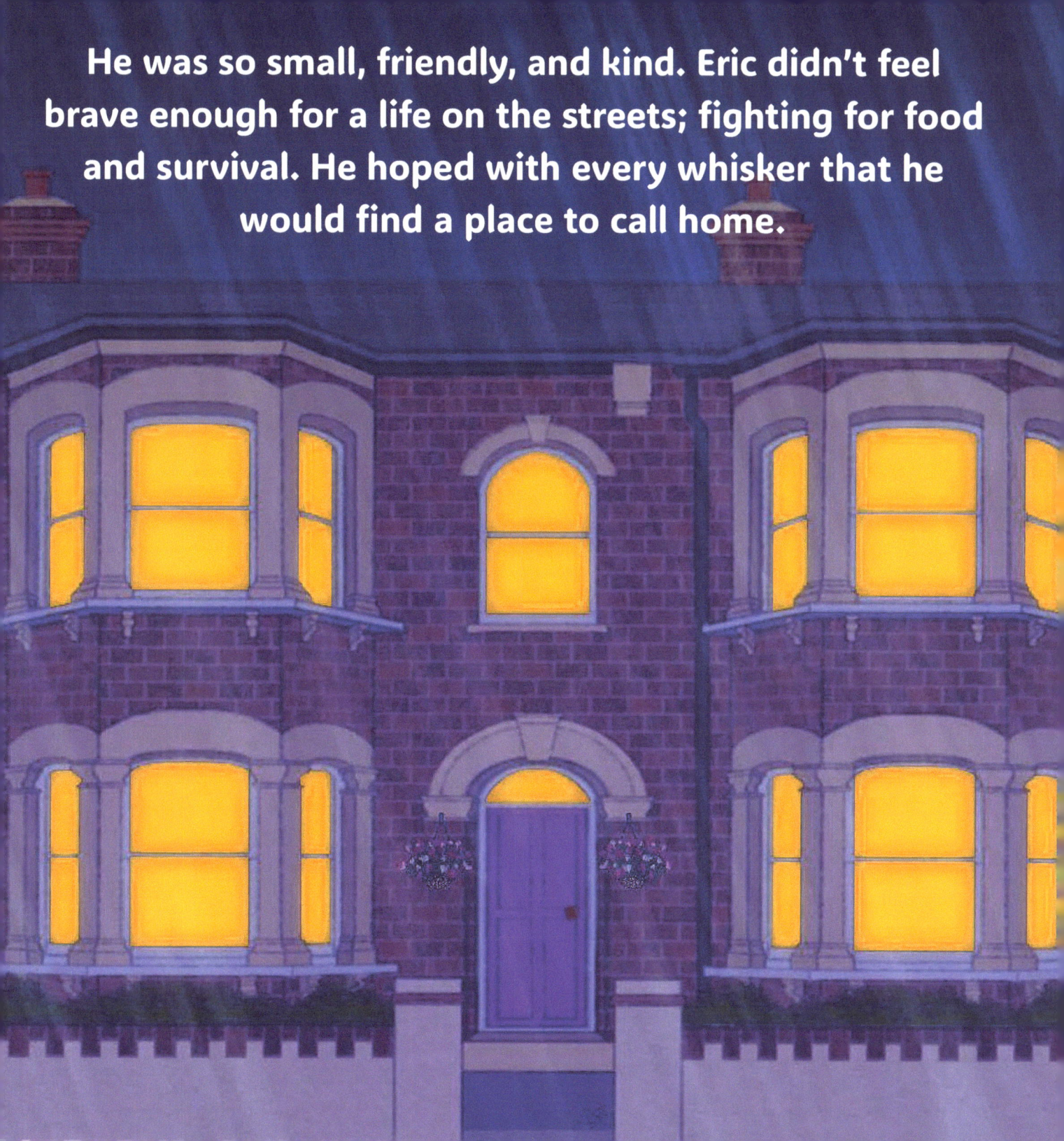

He was so small, friendly, and kind. Eric didn't feel brave enough for a life on the streets; fighting for food and survival. He hoped with every whisker that he would find a place to call home.

Life on the streets was lonely and dangerous. Eric spent the long hours of the day searching for shelter, food, and some love from a human.

His luck changed when Eric roamed further afield. He found a large back garden filled with bright flowers. Eric saw a striped hammock hanging by a tree to rest in.

Only being little, Eric used all his strength to jump into the hammock. As he landed, the hammock swung slightly, giving him a shock, before it stopped moving. Eric curled up on the soft material to rest, feeling content.

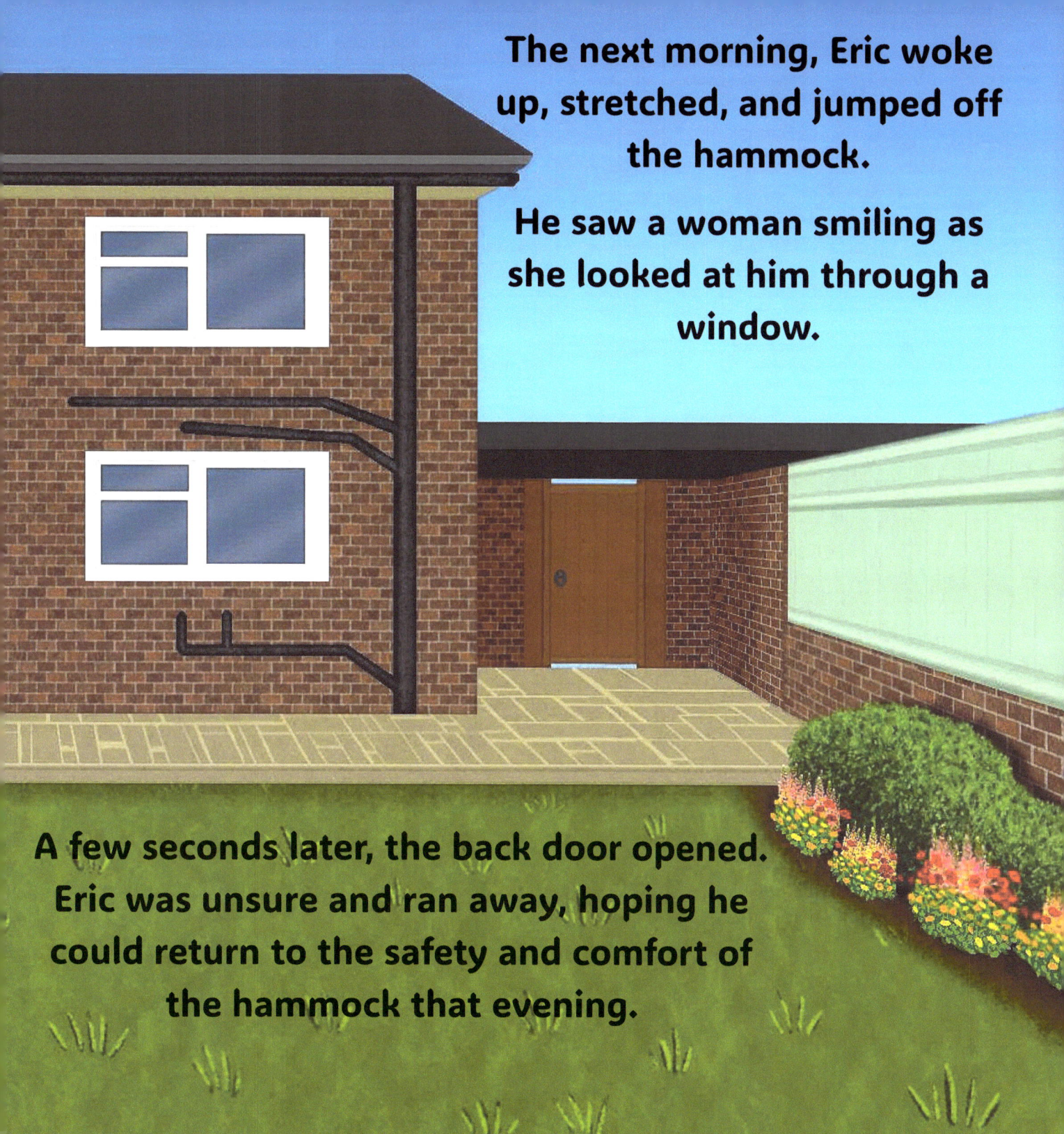

All day, Eric searched for food, wandered in gardens, and tried to make friends.
He ran from a dog twice, not an easy feat, as Eric only had little legs.

That evening, Eric returned to the same garden and did so the following evening. Some food had been placed on a plate for him beside the hammock. Eric gulped down the delicious food. It tasted like the best meal ever.

Perhaps this could be somewhere he could live? Somewhere he would be loved? For the next week, Eric returned every night to the garden with the hammock. Each night, food was left on a plate for him that he gobbled up.

A few days later, a woman came and picked him up. Eric didn't like being picked up, but the woman spoke in a soft voice and smiled.

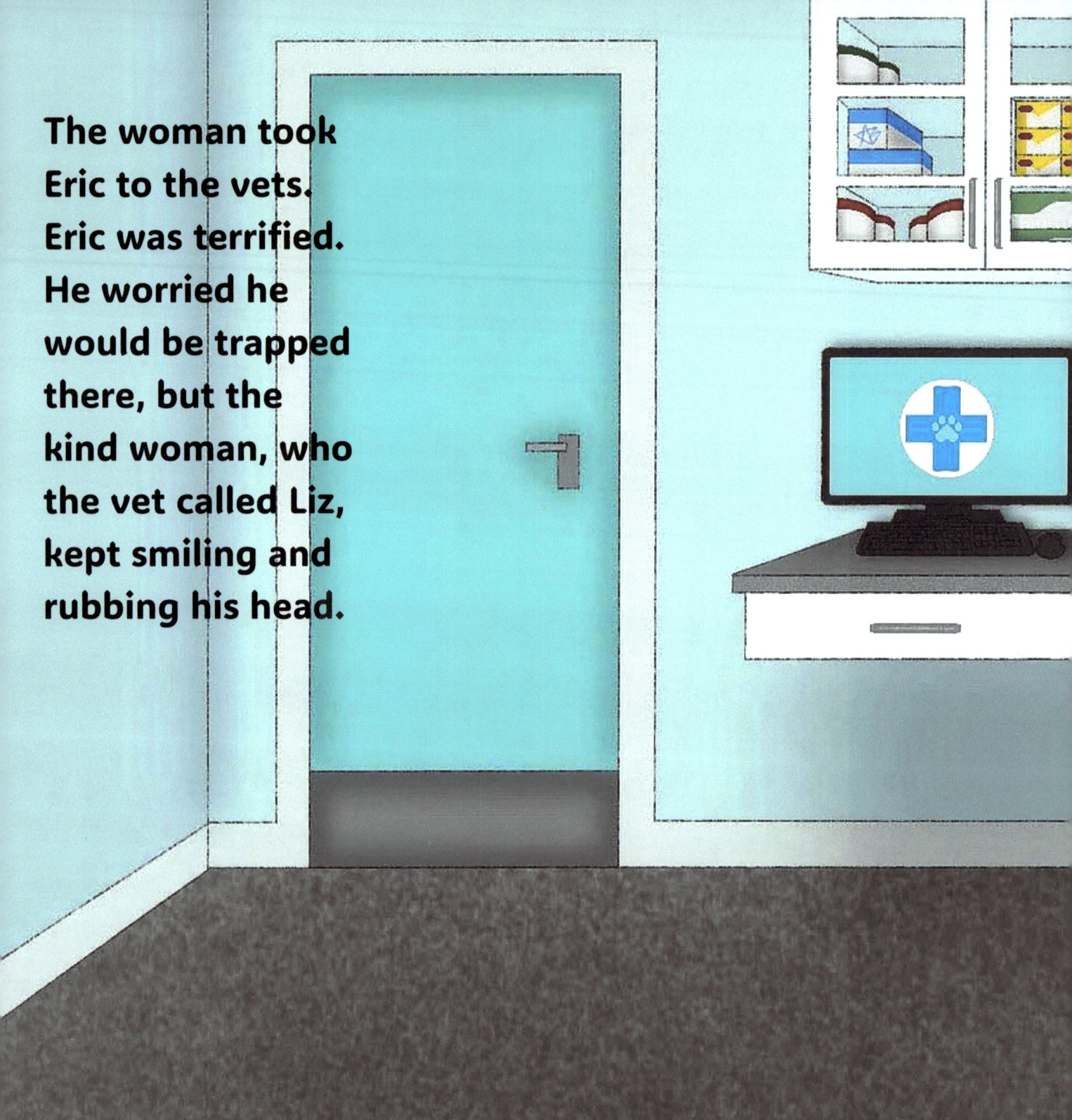

The woman took Eric to the vets. Eric was terrified. He worried he would be trapped there, but the kind woman, who the vet called Liz, kept smiling and rubbing his head.

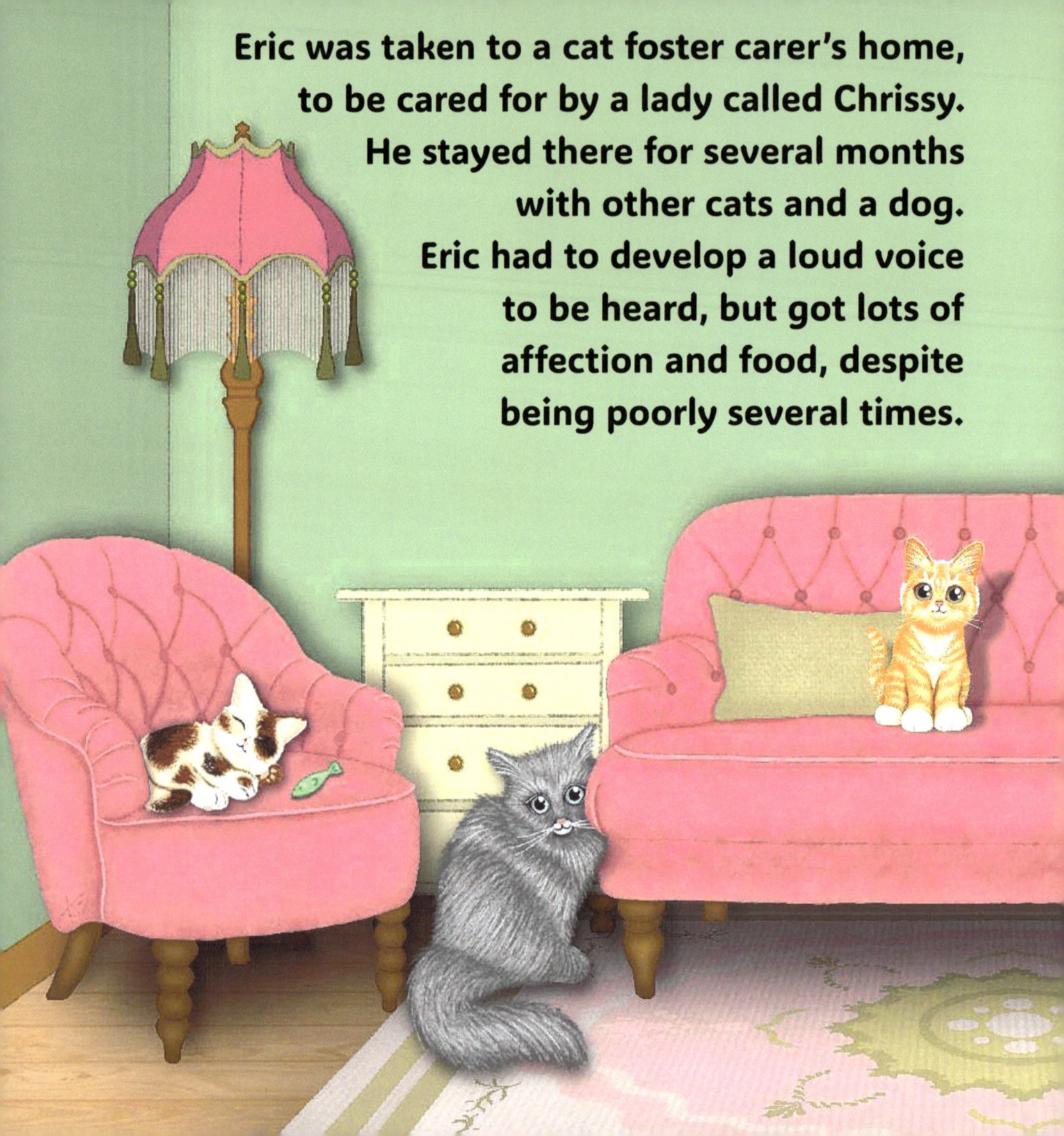

Eric was taken to a cat foster carer's home, to be cared for by a lady called Chrissy. He stayed there for several months with other cats and a dog. Eric had to develop a loud voice to be heard, but got lots of affection and food, despite being poorly several times.

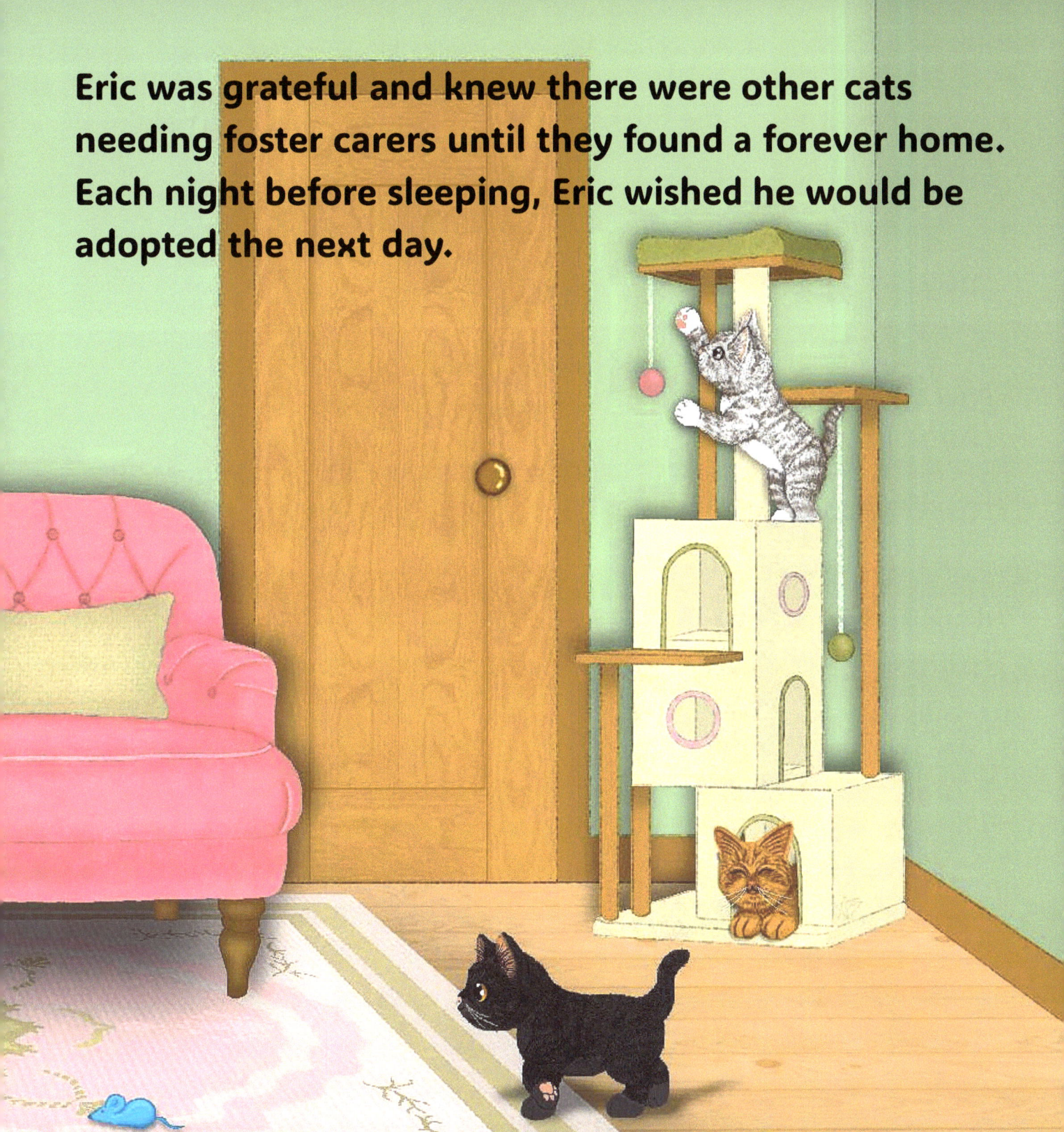

Eric was grateful and knew there were other cats needing foster carers until they found a forever home. Each night before sleeping, Eric wished he would be adopted the next day.

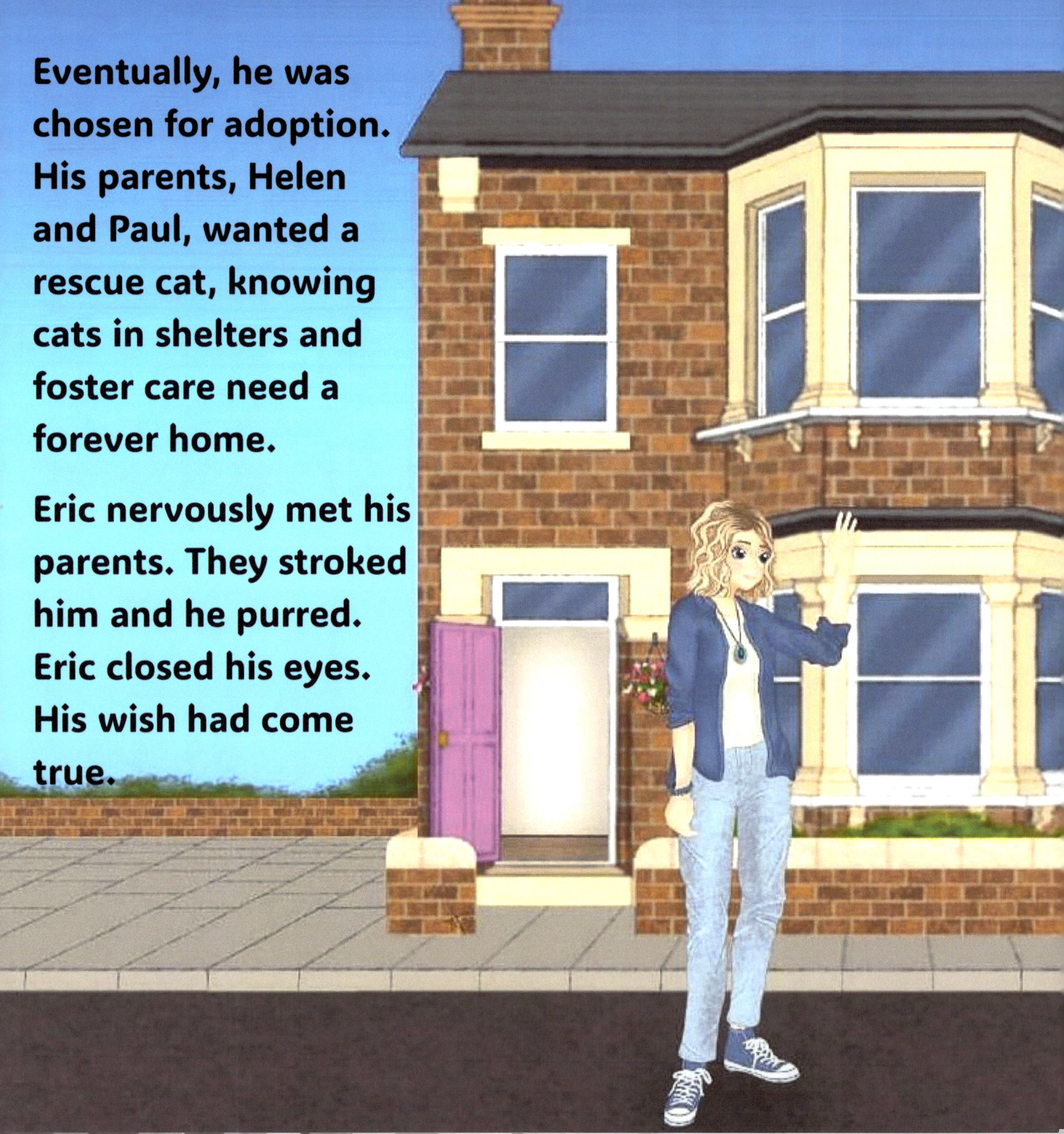

Eventually, he was chosen for adoption. His parents, Helen and Paul, wanted a rescue cat, knowing cats in shelters and foster care need a forever home.

Eric nervously met his parents. They stroked him and he purred. Eric closed his eyes. His wish had come true.

Helen and Paul took Eric home. Eric's new parents had everything he needed, including toys, beds, treats, and a large garden for him to explore. But most importantly, they had love to give to a cat, just like Eric had love to offer.

In that moment, Eric heard Newcastle United scoring a goal and felt his dad stroking him. It woke him up and brought him out of his dream.

He purred, stretched, and curled back around as his dad continued stroking him.

Eric never forgets how lucky he is to have been adopted by his parents. He tries to be a champion for rescue cats everywhere, wanting the world to adopt cats in need.

Eric now has his forever home, but still thinks about the many homeless cats needing love and safety and remembers his hard days on the streets.

Eric believes there is a home for every cat and a cat for every home. He is grateful each day that he and his parents found one another. His life is purr-fect, and now Eric will never be homeless again.

About Eric

Eric is six years old and found his forever home four and a half years ago with Helen and Paul. He is the boss of the house and makes his parents smile each day. Eric almost died three times with cat flu when he was a kitten. He is a survivor and is a happy, loving cat. Eric purrs constantly and loves to sit on a knee.

He is playful, still playing with his first ever toy; a tatty mouse called Scruffs and he likes to interrupt his mam when she is working, by sitting on her laptop.

He uses his social media platform to raise awareness of rescue cats and that there is a home for every cat.

Follow Eric on social media and find out about his daily escapades:

Instagram @erics_escapades_

X / Twitter @erics_escapades

TikTok @erics_escapades

New Beginnings Cat Rescue and Re-homing
Charity No. 1190655

New Beginnings are a small rescue and re-homing charity based in the North East of England. Volunteers at New Beginnings look after cats in their own homes that come to them as strays or that need re-homing for a variety of reasons. All cats are vaccinated, neutered and chipped prior to re-homing. New Beginnings home check all potential new owners and ask for an adoption fee to help continue their work.

New Beginnings are totally self-funded. Please visit their social media page for more information or if you wish to donate at New Beginnings Cat Rescue & Rehoming UK - Registered Charity number 1190655 | Facebook.

Helen Aitchison is an author from North East England. She writes adult fiction and works with charities and North East writers through her community interest company, Write on the Tyne.

www.helenaitchisonwrites.com   www.writeonthetyne.com

Acknowledgments

Thank you, reader, for buying this book and supporting rescue cats. We hope you enjoyed reading Eric's story and we are grateful your support will go towards assisting the charity that saved his life. Please leave a review for A Home for Every Cat if you enjoyed it and please check out New Beginnings Cat Rescue & Rehoming UK - Registered Charity number 1190655 | Facebook.

Thank you to Amelia for your beautiful illustrations that allowed us to create A Home for Every Cat and thank you to Holly and Eva for your input in the early days.

A massive thank you to New Beginnings, in particular Liz and Chrissy. Without your dedication to rescuing and re-homing cats in need, we would never have found Eric, who has brought us (and the world) so much love.

Big thanks to all of Eric's social media fans and to his grandparents for looking after him. And the most important thanks to Eric — a cat like no other that has the smallest legs, but the biggest heart.

All profits from the sale of this book are donated to New Beginnings Cat Rescue. Thank you for your support.

www.ingramcontent.com/pod-product-compliance
Lightning Source LLC
Chambersburg PA
CBHW041539040426
42446CB00002B/152